Masterpieces: Artists and Their Works

Van Gogh

by Shelley Swanson Sateren

W

FRANKLIN WATTS
LONDON • SYDNEY

This edition first published in 2004 by

Franklin Watts
96 Leonard Street
London
EC2A 4XD

Franklin Watts Australia
45–51 Huntley Street
Alexandria
NSW 2015

ISBN: 0 7496 5422 8

A CIP catalogue reference for this book is available from the British Library.

© Capstone Press 2002, 2004
Series created by Bridgestone Books, published by Capstone Press
151 Good Counsel Drive, P.O. Box 669, Mankato, Minnesota 56002

Printed in Hong Kong

Consultant: Joan Lingen, Ph.D. Professor of Art History, Clarke College, Iowa, USA

Cover Art: *Starry Night* (left) and *Self Portrait* (right) by Vincent Van Gogh

Editorial Credits
Blake Hoena, editor; Karen Risch, product planning editor; Heather Kindseth, cover and interior layout designer; Katy Kudela, photo researcher

Photo Credits
Art Resource/Musee d'Orsay, Paris, France, cover (right); Van Gogh Museum, Amsterdam, The Netherlands, 4, 12; Erich Lessing/Musee d'Orsay, Paris, France, 8 (top); Don Eastman, cover (left); Roget Viollet/Getty Images, 10 (bottom); Kunsthaus, Zurich, Switzerland/Bridgeman Art Library, 10 (top); Musee d'Orsay, Paris, France/Giraudon-Bridgeman Art Library, 20; National Gallery, London, UK/Bridgeman Art Library, 14; Philadelphia Museum of Art/CORBIS, 8 (bottom); Private Collection/Bridgeman Art Library, 6; Rijksmuseum Vincent Van Gogh, Amsterdam, The Netherlands/Bridgeman Art Library, 18; The Barnes Foundation, Merion, Pennsylvania, USA/Bridgeman Art Library, 16.

Table of Contents

Vincent painted *Self Portrait with Straw Hat* in 1887. His art style influenced Expressionism.

4

Vincent Van Gogh

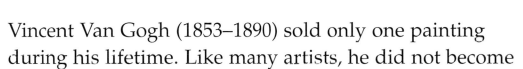

Vincent Van Gogh (1853–1890) sold only one painting during his lifetime. Like many artists, he did not become famous until after his death.

Vincent became an artist when he was 27 years old. He died ten years later. In that time, he created more than 1,000 paintings and drawings. He sometimes completed a painting in just one day.

Vincent tried to show emotions through his art. He often painted farmers and miners. He wanted to show the struggles of these working people. Vincent also had a unique painting style. His thick, curved brush strokes showed movement and excitement. This style of painting influenced **Expressionism**. During this art movement, people tried to show feelings in the art they created.

After his death, artists and art **critics** began to praise Vincent's work. People began to buy his paintings. Today, Vincent is one of the world's most famous painters. His paintings sell for millions of pounds.

Vincent made this charcoal drawing, *Portrait of Theodore Van Gogh*, of his father in 1881. It shows his father's seriousness.

Young Vincent

Vincent Willem Van Gogh was born in Groot Zundert, Holland, on 30th March 1853. His parents were called Theodore and Anna Cornelia Van Gogh. His father served as the minister for the small farming village where they lived.

Vincent was the oldest child in his family. He had three sisters and one brother, Theo. Theo was Vincent's closest friend. Vincent sometimes drew **sketches** of animals and plants that they saw while playing outside.

Vincent was a stubborn child. His moods often changed. Vincent's parents believed he was difficult and that he had rude manners. Vincent's behaviour created problems for him throughout his life.

Vincent's parents sent him to a boarding school when he was 12 years old. They wanted him to learn how to act and dress like a gentleman. However, he did not keep himself or his clothes tidy at school. He also argued with other students. At the age of 15, Vincent left school to find a job.

Vincent learned how to paint by copying Millet's works in his own style. *La Siete, d'apres Millet*, or *The Meridian* (top) is Vincent's painting. Millet painted *Meridian* (bottom).

Early Influences

In 1869, Vincent began to work as an assistant for an art gallery. His uncle was an art dealer and Vincent took a job with his company, Goupil & Cie.

At first, Vincent was successful at his job. He enjoyed seeing art and discussing it with other people. In 1873, he moved to London to work for the company's art gallery there.

Vincent eventually became unhappy with his job. He did not get along with the other workers and he sometimes argued with customers about the paintings they wanted to buy. In 1876, Vincent decided to leave the company.

While in England, Vincent studied art and books. He admired English writers such as Charles Dickens, who wrote about working-class people.

The French painter Jean-François Millet also influenced Vincent. Vincent studied Millet's paintings of peasants working in fields. Soon, Vincent began to draw and paint people at work.

Vincent's letters to Theo included sketches of people he saw. He liked to draw and paint working people such as in *Two Peasants Planting Potatoes* (top).

Borinage

In 1876, Vincent entered school to become a priest like his father. However, he had trouble with his studies and failed his exams.

Vincent did not let this failure stop him. In 1879, he convinced church officials to allow him to be a minister in Borinage, a coal-mining region in southern Belgium.

The coal miners there were very poor. They had little food and lived in wooden shacks. Vincent felt sorry for them and he often gave them his extra clothing and food. Unfortunately, the church officials at the time did not approve of these actions. They told Vincent he had to leave his job.

During his time in Borinage, Vincent often wrote to Theo. In his letters, he included sketches showing the miners' struggles.

Vincent began to draw more after he left his job as a priest. He wrote to Theo saying that creating art made him feel less sad and lonely. At the age of 27, Vincent decided that he wanted to be an artist.

In 1885, Vincent painted *Potato Eaters*. This painting is considered to be his first masterpiece. Vincent used dark colours such as browns and greys in many of his early paintings.

Beginnings as an Artist

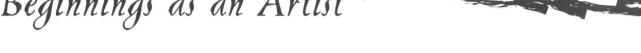

In 1880, Vincent moved to Brussels, Belgium, to study art. He created many pencil and charcoal drawings of nature scenes and peasants working.

In 1882, Vincent began to experiment with oil paints. He sometimes squeezed paint out of the tube right onto the painting. Vincent was excited about his art and would often paint all day and into the night.

Theo helped Vincent become an artist. He sent Vincent money for art supplies and sent art books that he could study. The money Theo gave him was the only money Vincent had. It was not always enough to buy both art supplies and food, so he often went hungry. To Vincent, art supplies were more important than food.

Vincent was unable to earn money selling his paintings. He painted poor people because he wanted to show their struggles. However, in those days, people did not want to buy paintings of people at work. They wanted to see more pleasant scenes.

Sunflowers were Vincent's favourite flowers. He painted seven different versions of *Sunflowers*.

Paris

In 1886, Vincent moved to Paris to live with Theo. In Paris, many artists were experimenting with new styles of art. Vincent wanted to meet these painters and discuss art with them.

At the time, **Impressionism** was a popular art movement. **Impressionists** tried to paint scenes as they appeared at a quick glance. These artists used broken brush strokes to do this.

Vincent also became interested in Japanese art while in Paris. Japanese artists used bright colours.

Impressionism and Japanese art were both big influences on Vincent's own art work. He began to use short, curved brush strokes. He also stopped painting with dark colours and began to use brighter colours instead. Yellow became one of his favourites.

Vincent was still unable to sell his paintings. He often had no money to hire models whom he could paint, so he ended up painting more than 20 **self portraits**.

Joseph-Etienne Roulin was a postman in the town of Arles.

He was one of Vincent's only friends there.

Arles

Living with Vincent was hard for Theo. Vincent made a huge mess and often argued. In February 1888, Vincent moved to a small village in southern France called Arles. He moved so he would stop fighting with Theo, but he also wanted to paint the scenery there.

Vincent continued to paint in bright colours and curl his brush strokes. Their curved shapes added motion and excitement to his paintings. Later, Vincent's style of painting would help influence Expressionism.

Vincent wanted to start an artists' community in Arles. He invited other artists to join him. Only Paul Gauguin visited. Vincent and Gauguin discussed art and painted together. But they often disagreed and argued about art.

After one argument, Gauguin was very angry with Vincent. Gauguin decided to leave Arles. Vincent was so upset that he cut off a piece of his own left ear.

Wheatfield with Crows was one of Vincent's last paintings. Some people believe that the dark sky shows how angry and upset Vincent was at the time.

Illness

Vincent struggled throughout his life. He often had no money for food. Many experts believe that Vincent suffered from a mental illness, or that he had **epilepsy**. He often had attacks, during which he did not know what he was doing. Another theory is that he suffered from lead poisoning, which can gradually damage the brain. At the time, lead was used in paints.

In 1889, Vincent stayed in a mental-health hospital. He continued to paint there, but he still had attacks. He struggled with feelings of sadness and loneliness and even painting did not make him feel happy.

In 1890, Vincent moved to the village of Auvers near Paris. He wanted to be closer to Theo. In Auvers, Vincent was under the care of Dr. Paul Gachet.

Soon after Vincent moved, he learned that Theo might lose his job as an art dealer. Vincent felt guilty. Theo had always given him money and now he felt as if he was a burden to his brother.

Vincent painted this portrait, *Dr. Paul Gachet*, in 1890.
It is one of his most famous paintings.

Vincent Van Gogh's Art

The news that Theo might lose his job upset Vincent a great deal. On 27th July, 1890, Vincent shot himself. He died two days later at the age of 37. Theo was extremely saddened by his brother's death and died within six months.

Theo's wife, Johanna, took care of Vincent's art and the letters he wrote to Theo. Stacks of Vincent's paintings filled Johanna's apartment. She shared them with museums and had Vincent's letters published in books.

About 25 years after Vincent's death, people began to admire his art. Today, he is one of the most famous painters of all time, and many museums around the world display his art.

In 1987, Vincent's painting *Irises* sold for $54 million (roughly £34 million). In 1990, his painting *Dr. Paul Gachet* sold for $82.5 million (roughly £52 million). These paintings are some of the most expensive ever sold.

Timeline

1853 – Vincent is born in Groot Zundert on 30th March.

1857 – Vincent's brother, Theo, is born.

1869 – Vincent begins to work for Goupil & Cie.

1873 – Vincent moves to London.

1879 – Vincent becomes a priest in Borinage.

1880 – Vincent decides to become an artist; he moves to Brussels to study art.

1886 – Vincent moves to Paris to live with Theo.

1888 – Vincent moves to Arles; Paul Gauguin visits Vincent; the two artists discuss art and paint together.

1889 – Vincent stays in a mental-health hospital in St. Remy.

1890 – Vincent moves to Auvers.

1890 – Vincent dies on 27th July.

1891 – Theo dies on 25th January.

Useful Websites

www.vangoghmuseum.nl
This is the official website for the Van Gogh museum in Holland. It includes an excellent range of his works of art and takes visitors on a virtual tour of the galleries.

www.van-gogh-art.co.uk
This is a fascinating website which includes a detailed Van Gogh biography, a study of his painting techniques, examples of his famous works of art and copies of his letters to his brother.

www.bbc.co.uk/arts/impressionism/step_vangogh.shtml
This fun, interactive website gives step by step instructions on how to create your own Van Gogh painting. Photographs are used at each stage, as visual guides.

www.whytownps.sa.edu.au/visarts/
This Australian school website looks at many different artists, including Impressionists, and explores their various styles of art. It also provides a range of art activities and quizzes.

www.vangoghgallery.com
A fully comprehensive website exploring Van Gogh's life as an artist. It includes photographs of the Van Gogh family and other important people in Van Gogh's life.

Note to parents and teachers
Every effort has been made by the Publishers to ensure that these websites are suitable for children; that they are of the highest educational value, and that they contain no inappropriate or offensive material. However, because of the nature of the Internet, it is impossible to guarantee that the contents of these sites will not be altered. We strongly advise that Internet access is supervised by a responsible adult.

Glossary

critic – someone who reviews art, books or films
epilepsy – a mental illness that causes people to have blackouts or convulsions
Expressionism – an art movement in which artists tried to show emotions in their work
Impressionism – an art style in which broken brush strokes are used to paint a scene the way it looks at a quick glance
Impressionists – artists who use the style of Impressionism
self portrait – a piece of artwork which an artist creates of himself or herself
sketch – a rough drawing of something

Index